2nd To Flavored Memories Of The Soul

VOLUME 1

SYLVERTOOTH

authorHOUSE®

AuthorHouse™
1663 Liberty Drive
Bloomington, IN 47403
www.authorhouse.com
Phone: 1-800-839-8640

First published by AuthorHouse 10/21/2009

ISBN: 978-1-4490-3683-6 (sc)

Printed in the United States of America
Bloomington, Indiana

This book is printed on acid-free paper.

1. What is? IF IT DON'T KILL U IT GOT TO CURE U

My Meaning: taking something that you feel that you should not take.

2. What is? I AM SICK OF U

My Meaning: that person is getting on my nerves

3. What is? YOUR SO DAMN EXTREME

My Meaning: a person that takes everything to the limit

4. What is? YOUR OUT OF ORDER

My Meaning: doing or saying something that is incorrect at the time

5. What is? YOUR SO SILLY

My Meaning: someone that does something funny

(Just a thought) MY GRANDDAUTHER SAID O GRANNY U BUYING DIAPERS
FOR YOUR PANTIES diapers for adults

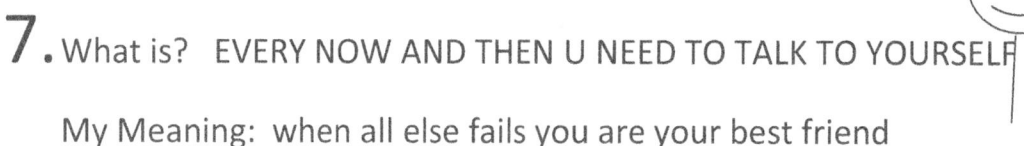

6. What is? WHEN I WALK AWAY

My Meaning: Leaving

7. What is? EVERY NOW AND THEN U NEED TO TALK TO YOURSELF

   My Meaning: when all else fails you are your best friend

8. What is? YOUR SILLY ASS

My Meaning: doing something real stupid

9. What is?   YOU CAN'T TAKE CARE OF A BIG WOUND WITH A LITTLE BANDAID

My Meaning: trying to fix something that is way too big

10.   What is?   WHEREVER YOU MAY BE LET YOUR GAS GO FREE

My Meaning: DON'T HOLD FARTS IN

1. What is?   MAKE IT PURR TREAT IT RIGHT LADIES

   My Meaning: treat the viginal like a newborn baby

2. What is?   THIS IS SOME BULL SHIT HERE

   My Meaning: Being put on hold with the phone company hours at a time

3. What is?   LET YOUR HAIR DOWN

   My Meaning: Get comfortable

4. What is? MY BAD

   My Meaning: just an apology

5. What is? DAMN DID YOU SEE THAT My Meaning: something happen in front of you and you are wondering did anyone else see it

(Just a thought) Where is the beauty…in the booty?

Where is the beauty in the booty? Is it round enough for you? Is it firm enough for you? Or is it soft as cotton? Is it apple round from the behind or sharply fine brown? Is it a brick house stacked or is it a little under proportioned? Take your pick in the beauty of the booty all shapes and sizes, depending on what you like or don't like. So when you see girls backside finds some beauty in that booty because beauty is in the eyes of the beholder so hold on to your

Your beauty in the booty, everybody should have one, and now a days you go buy you one any shape or size, but it would be nice if you could keep it real.

1. What is? DROP IT LIKE ITS HOT

   My Meaning: how far can you go? Down to the floor!

2. What is? SO WHAT THAT MEAN

   My Meaning: make yourself clear

3. What is? I AM NOT GOING TO BE there

   My Meaning: people that you don't want to be bother with

4. What is? IF I SEE HIM I'LL LET YOU KNOW

   My Meaning: are you looking for that other person

5. What is? HEAD MAN

My Meaning: a man know who know what to do with the virginal

1. What is? EYE CANDY

   My Meaning: when a gay man sees something he likes

2. What is? TO LOOSE

   My Meaning: not being much of a lady

3. What is? MY TIME YOUR DIME

   My Meaning: if you willing to pay I'll talk

4. What is? LOCK DOWN

   My Meaning: everything is at a halt

5. What is? YOUR LOOKING KIND OF JAZZY

   My Meaning: something my mother use to say

(Just a thought) A HELL HOLE

Every time I cone to my peoples house why is it that they feel they have to fight or argue. I don't need this mess in my life. I have enough drama in my own life. I need peace and harmony in my life I have had enough "shit" arguing, fighting, confusing, and unnecessary B.S. so please explain to me why it is? When I come to visit someone feel they have to argue and fight. Are you trying to send a message to me? Maybe? I am seeking peace and it seems like its hard to find but once I come into my own, I can control my own environment and make my comfort zone into what I want it to be.

1. What is? I'M SOMEONE YOU SHOULD KNOW

My Meaning: that person is doing something special and he wants you to know it

2. What is? U MY NIGGER IF YOU DON'T GET NO BIGGER

My Meaning: you my friend

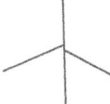

3. What is? SHUT IT DOWN

My Meaning: stop now

4. What is? KICK BACK

My Meaning: relax

5. What is? ONE UP ON U

My Meaning: I tricked you

1. What is? I'AM JUST AROUND THE CONNER

My Meaning: someone calls and tells you that they are just around the corner but they are lying

2. What is? U ARE GOING TO BE A NERVES WRECK IF U DON'T STOP WORRING

My Meaning: just keep a positive outlook

3. What is? YOU GOT IT GOING ON

My Meaning: we look good

4. What is? YOUR SMOKIN

My Meaning: your body looks goods

5. What is? GIRL DID YOU HERE ABOUT THAT

My Meaning: gossip

1. What is? I'AM ONLY ONE PERSON

My Meaning: somebody that doesn't want to be pulled 5 different ways

2. What is? WHATS POPIN

My Meaning: What's going on?

3. What is? YOU SHIT OUT OF LUCK

My Meaning: you missed out

4. What is? EXCUSE ME

My Meaning: I'm kindly asking you to move out of my way

5. What is? I'AM SORRY

My Meaning: I didn't mean to do that

(Just a thought)

If you say you're sorry you will be sorry for the rest of your life

1. What is?   PARTEN ME

My Meaning: Getting the hell out of my way

2. What is?   STOP CALLING MY NAME

My Meaning: someone is constantly calling my name and they don't want shit

3. What is?   WHAT'S KICKEN

My Meaning: What's happening?

4. What is? BIG PIMPIN

My Meaning: person with nice possessions

5. What is? THAT'S CRAZY

My Meaning: someone's doing something that doesn't make any sense

(Wisdom is power)

Makes a lot of sense

1. What is?   GET OUT OF MY ASS

   My Meaning: whenever you driving and the car behind you seems like it's glued to you back bumper

2. What is?   GET OFF BACK OFF

   My Meaning: leave me alone. Get away, stay away

3. What is?   THIS IS NOT WORKING

   My Meaning: something isn't right

4. What is?   DON'T TOUCH ME RIGHT NOW

   My Meaning: get your hands off of me

5. What is?   MY FEET HURT ME SO BAD

   My Meaning: u been standing on them to long

"The boom boom room "

Meet me at the boom boom room , we can have fun, laughs a few drinks, talk about old times ,shot the breeze, lie, unfortunate about past events, old events, boyfriends , and how we used to be , the way we used to look , and how we used to get down , down , down !! And how we are getting high to the (sky) drinking, and thinking smoking and chocking, doping and moping how what is in your future? Clicking, clacking, sometimes nicking, flying and lying, hoping, and moping not thinking about your future. Well hell, don't you think you should make a change; things should not stay the same, do a check up from the neck up start being more positive about what you are saying and doing.

"Why I a label a bad girl?"

Why am I labeling a bad girl? Is it because you think you know me?

Or what I have done or did in the past, and the people I am going out with, the people I party with , the people that is in my circle of entertainment for years ?, and what we did then , and what we are doing now . Who are you to be so dame judgmental of when your ass is doing everything that you can think of and some big enough to do, o hell nall!! you can't be saying that I am a bad girl , while your ass is a under cover lover , smoking, doping, , chocking licking , and lacking and crying out praise the lord and its spirit contents. Get real we are all God's children and people so don't try to find the bad in me and you don't see the bad in yourself it's not your world it is God's and you better know it !!

1.   What is? I'AM TRYING TO GIVE U SOME

      My Meaning: its here for the taking but you not making a move

2.   What is? I PULL ALL YOUR PLUGS OUT

   My Meaning: someone who uses their authority to make your life fucking hell

3.   What is? YOU CAUGHT ME WITH MY DREWS DOWN

    My Meaning: someone catches u off guard

4.   What is? TUTTA' TA

My Meaning: virginal pussy etc etc etc

5.   What is? ARE YOU FREE TONIGHT

   My Meaning: what r u do

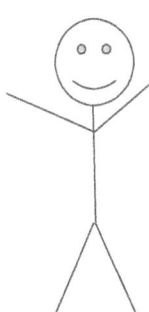

1. What is? ALL HE SEE IS $ SIGN

My Meaning: if u don't have money then he not feeling u

2. What is? I HEAR U

My Meaning: this person is listening to u and understanding what u r saying

3. What is? I KNOW YOU WANT TO KILL ME FOR BEING LATE

My Meaning: that person is so late it is a thousand things u could have been doing

4. What is? O-WOW

My Meaning: the things that people say

5. What is? U THINK

My Meaning: someone answers their own questions

1. What is? BEAT IT

   My Meaning: get away from me

2. What is? BLOW ME

   My Meaning: someone says something stupid and u can't slap the shit out of them

3. What is? THERE'S ALWAYS TODAY TOMORROW AND THE NEXT DAY

   My Meaning: then what are u waiting for

4. What is? I'AM LEAKING

   My Meaning: a woman who is having her monthly

5. What is? GIVE ME SOME OF THAT

   My Meaning: begging ass people

1. What is? AM NOT FEELING GOOD

My Meaning: your body is trying to shut down

2. What is? SAY IT ANT SO

My Meaning: someone tell u something that u can't believe

3. What is? IT'S GOING ON

My Meaning: someone is telling u about something u shouldn't miss

4. What is? ARE YOU FREE TONIGHT

My Meaning: r u available

5. What is? HOW LONG HAS IT BEEN

My Meaning: a person who u have not seen in years

Thanks

I thank you for being so good to me , loving, taking care of me ,protecting keeping me being their for (me)in my (darkness hour) understanding me inspire of my shortcomings , you are my sunshine on(rainy days) you are my warmth when I feel cold despair you're my friend in a time of need my mother, father, bother sister , when it seem know one understand or care , but you do so think you again even for being their for me when sometimes it seems like I am standing alone (I know it not true) thanks, thanks and many and many more to you

1. What is? YOU GOT A LOT OF BALLS

My Meaning: someone does something u can't believe him or her is doing

2. What is? I GOT YOUR # NUMBER

My Meaning: I'll let my book reader answer this one

3. What is? TELL IT LIKE IT IS

My Meaning: someone telling something u feels like   that's the truth

4. What is? YOU THINK WE CAN DO SOMETHING

My Meaning: wanting to do something with another person

5. What is? GIRL CALL ME BACK

My Meaning: to busy to talk right now

1. What is? FILL IN THE BLANKS ————————

Putting an end to the guessing.

2. What is? ONE THING AT A TIME ◊

My Meaning: u can only put one shoe at a time

3. What is? HOLD ON ONE MOMENT AM THINKING ABOUT IT ☺

My Meaning: u ask someone something that u want an answer to right a way

4. What is? I GOT TO TAKE A CHILL PILL ⧖

My Meaning: you're doing too much

5. What is? INDECENT AND IN ORDER

My Meaning: correctly done ♡

1. What is? ALL THE TIME that WE PUT IN this WAS SOME BULL SHIT

My Meaning: u did something and it did not work out.

What is? TIME THEIVES

My Meaning: someone taking time from u

2. What is? IT'S HOW YOU DO NOT WHAT YOU DO

My Meaning: your action speaks louder then words you the reader can help with this one]

3. What is? IT'S A TIME AND PLACE FOR EVERY THING

My Meaning: someone is doing something in appropriate in a inappropriate place

4. What is? AN OPINION IS LIKE A ASS HOLE EVERYONE HAS ONE

My Meaning: your suggestion is not always right

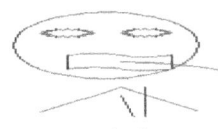

1. What is? I DID'NT THINK TWICE

My Meaning: this was done right away

2. What is? WATCH WHAT YOU SAY

My Meaning: don't say the wrong thing around the wrong person

3. What is? HE'S MY FAVORITE

My Meaning: making a statement about how you feel about someone

4. What is? DO IT TO IT HURT

My Meaning: maximize

5. What is? THIS IS FOR THE NEEDY NOT THE GREEDY

My Meaning: someone who has a lot already and want much much more

1. What is? HOLD THAT THOUGHT

My Meaning: we're thinking at the same time

2. What is? JUST MAKE ME

My Meaning: demanding I do somethin

3. What is? I DON'T WANT TO HURT YOU

My Meaning: is what a nigger is saying when he about to leave your ass

4. What is? GIVE ME SOME LOVE

My Meaning: someone u enjoy seeing

5. What is? IT'S WHAT IT IS

My Meaning: your settling for something u don't want to

1. What is? YOU DON'T KNOW ME

My Meaning: don't think you know the personality when u barely know the person

2. What is? THAT'S A BULL SHIT TIP YOU GAVE ME

My Meaning: doing something that someone told that this is so great

3. What is? GIRL CONTROL YOU EMOTIONS

My Meaning: stop crying over that raggedy ass nigger

4. What is? TRUST ME

My Meaning: believe in that person

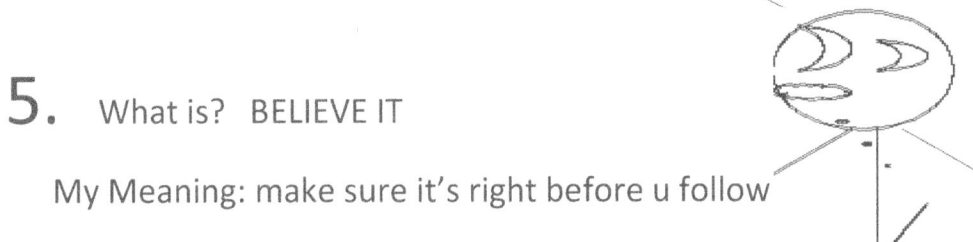

5. What is? BELIEVE IT

My Meaning: make sure it's right before u follow

1. What is?   YOU LOOK LIKE A FOOL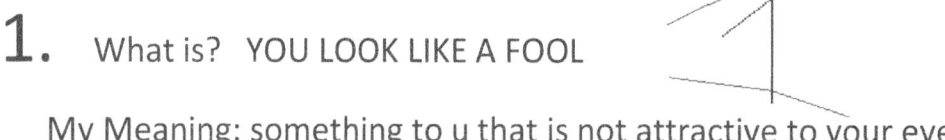

My Meaning: something to u that is not attractive to your eye

2. What is?   MAYBE IT'S MEANT FOR YOU TO GO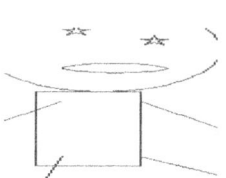

My Meaning: premention

3. What is?   THAT'S YOUR ASS

My Meaning: you're in trouble now

4. What is?   ITS HOW YOU TREAT ME

My Meaning: it's the way u talk to me or how u act towards me

5. What is?   THAT WAS A DOPE FIEND MOVE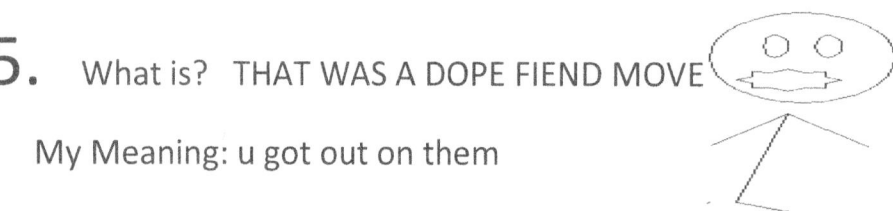

My Meaning: u got out on them

1. What is? GIVE ME THE USELRAL

   My Meaning: getting the same thing all the time

2. What is? YOU WHERE ON MY MIND

   My Meaning: think about that one person

3. What is? IT'S HERE SOME WHERE

   My Meaning: it's not in the spot u thought u put it in

4. What is? TAKE ME TO THE NEXT LEV

   My Meaning: I want to go higher

5. What is? A,B,C YOUR WAY OUT

   My Meaning: stay out of our conversation

1. What is? DON'T FEED INTO IT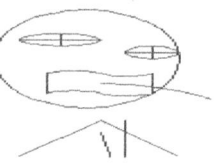

My Meaning: don't make more of it then

2. What is? IS HOGMALLS NUTS

My Meaning: yes they r

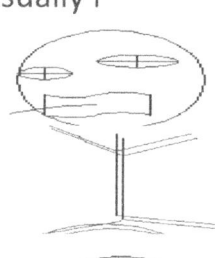

3. What is? STOP PUTTING ME LAST AND PUT ME FIRST

My Meaning: be their for me more then u usually r

4. What is? BITCH GET MY MONEY

My Meaning: pimp mentality

5. What is? YOU HAVE A PIMP MENTALTY

My Meaning: u demand everything

1. What is? TWO THINGS YOU ARE GOING TO do is STAY BLACK AND DIE

   My Meaning: two things that r certain [death and taxes]

2. What is? A HOUSE IS NOT A HOME

   My Meaning: a house is not a home if u have rigged ass people live in it

3. What is? I WAS THE GOOD GUY

   My Meaning: u did all u could

4. What is? YOU ALWAYS TRYING TO IMPRESS SOMEBODY

   My Meaning: try to always be ass kisser

5. What is? GIRL IM BACK AT HOME

   My Meaning: it wasn't so hot out their after all

1. What is?   ARE YOU OK

My Meaning: let's talk

2. What is?   WHAT'S WRONG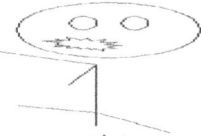

My Meaning: I'll let the reader answer this one

3. What is?   THAT AIN'T RIGHT

My Meaning: your rigged ass is wrong

4. What is?   HE'S ON THE MONEY

My Meaning: right on time

5. What is?   TOO SHORT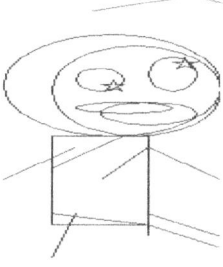

My Meaning: need more time

1. What is? SOMETIMES THEY LIVE FOREVER

   My Meaning: roaches

2. What is? PRESS ON

   My Meaning: never stop

3. What is? IS PIG PUSSY PORK

   My Meaning: yes

4. What is? NEXT WEEK SOMETIME

   My Meaning: do it another time

5. What is? COME BACK

   My Meaning: right now is not a good time

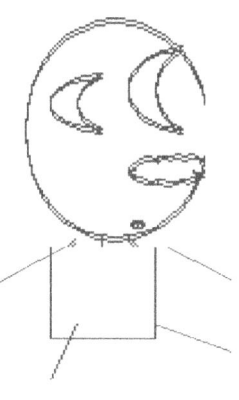

1. What is?   STOP GETTING IN MY HEAD

    My Meaning: quit tell me this bullshit

2. What is?   IT'S FREE

    My Meaning: O

3. What is?   GIVE IT RIGHT BACK

    My Meaning: soon

4. What is?   HEAD SHOT

My Meaning: lick upside the head

5. What is?   NIGGA WHAT

My Meaning: not believing something that a person said

1. What is? AM THE C,E,O OF WHAT

   My Meaning: any fucking thing u want to be

2. What is? THERE WON'T BE A NEXT TIME

   My Meaning: if your silly ass keep acting the way u keep acting

3. What is? IS YOUR MOTHER MADE OF GLASS

   My Meaning: get the hell from in front of me I can't see

4. What is? HANDLE YOUR BUSINESS

   My Meaning: Does what u need to do

5. What is? DID I ANSWER YOUR QUESTION

   My Meaning: no

1. What is? MOMMY A FEW MORE MINS

My Meaning: mom I am doing something that you can't see and I'm almost done   give me five min.

2. What is? GIVING YOU MY THOUGHTS

My Meaning: speak you mind

3. What is? RESPECT ME

My Meaning: treat me with the dignity I deserve

4. What is? WHAT THE HELL IS THIS

My Meaning: good question

5. What is? GOD TAKES CARE OF BABIES OLD FOLKS AND DAMN FOOLS

My Meaning: God don't like people between age of 6 and 60

1. What is? THAT'S IT I'M OUTTA HERE

    My Meaning: leaving'

2. What is? SEE YA

    My Meaning: later

3. What is? DAMN RIGHT

    My Meaning: making a powerful statement that u feel is right

4. What is? IM NOT FEELING YOU

    My Meaning: I don't see the same thing in u as I saw before

5. What is? YOU FEEL ME

    My Meaning: u understand

1. What is?   DO HATE PARTICIPATE

My Meaning: don't be jealous towards my success get your own

2. What is?   YOU GOT BALLS DOING WHAT YOU ARE DOING

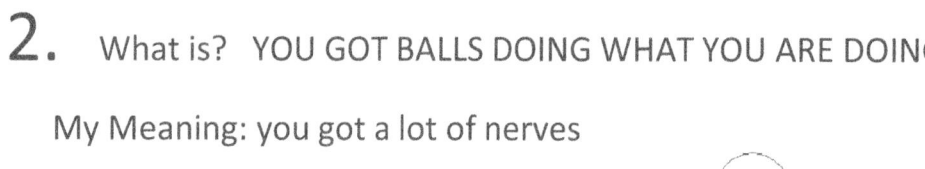

My Meaning: you got a lot of nerves

3. What is? CHECK OUT TIME

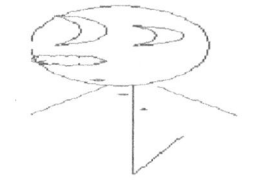

My Meaning: leave

4. What is?   LAST CALL

My Meaning: no more

5. What is?   I CAN'T AFFORD

My Meaning: Too much money

1. What is? RACCON EYES

My Meaning: two black eyes

2. What is? HE WANTS IT BAD

My Meaning: hungry for it

3. What is? WERE MISSING EACH OTHER

My Meaning: need to get back together

4. What is? HE'S CLEAN AS THE BOARD OF HEALTH

My Meaning: he's dresses sharp or {he free of disease}

5. What is? YOU WANT A LITTLE NIBBLE

My Meaning: sexual slang

1. What is?   BOTTOM OF MY FEET TO THE TOP OF MY HEAD

   My Meaning: what

2. What is?   NUMNUT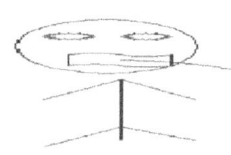

   My Meaning: dummy

3. What is?   WHAT ARE YOU PLANNING TO DO

   My Meaning: not a dam thing

4. What is?   IT'S BEEN ONE

   My Meaning: it over with [it a warp]

5. What is?   EVERYBODY WITH A EXTRA LEG IS NOT A MAN

   My Meaning: they might be a woman

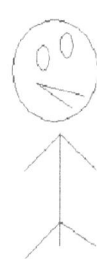

1. What is? MAKE ME WHOLE

   My Meaning: complete me my brother

2. What is? KEEP YOUR LEGS CLOSE AND YOUR DRESS DOWN

   My Meaning: something my mother used to say to keep from having sex [it didn't work]

3. What is? ARE THOSE FAKE

   My Meaning: I don't know, squeeze them and see.

4. What is? IS THAT REAL

   My Meaning: yes

5. What is? STOP WHILE YOU AHEAD

   My Meaning: you're pushing to hard

1. What is? STOP THE MADDNESS

    My Meaning: stop that entire yin yang you spitting' out you dome piece son

2. What is? NOT NOW MAYBE LATER

    My Meaning: hell naw never

3. What is? IM ALL NATRUAL

    My Meaning: on down to my feet

4. What is? IF AT FIRST YOU DON'T SUCCED WHAT IN THE HELL SHOULD YOU DO

    My Meaning: keep on trying

5. What is? THINK WITH YOUR BRAIN AND NOT YOUR DICK

    My Meaning: use my smarts not my body

1.   What is?   LET ME TOUCH YOU THERE

My Meaning: sexual innuendos

2.   What is?   THAT WAS A GOOD DAY

My Meaning: better than the last one

3.   What is?   LET ME TASTE YOUR HONEY

My Meaning: let me drink that p#$$y juice ☺

4.   What is?   LET ME HIT THE SPLIT

My Meaning: let me tear that up some more ☺

5.   What is? LET ME HIT THE CHERRY

My Meaning: let me break the wall that blocks my love from entering your whole body ☺

1. What is? LET ME HIT THE SPOT

   My Meaning: virgina

2. What is? POUTIG

   My Meaning: virgina

3. What is? COTACAT

   My Meaning: virgina

4. What is? COON

   My Meaning: virgina

5. What is? SPLIT

   My Meaning: virgina

1. What is? MUFFEN

   My Meaning: nick name for p-s-y or what ever u want it to be

2. What is? LET'S SEE

   My Meaning: what it is

3. What is? ALL EYES ON ME

   My Meaning: I just want u to look at me

4. What is? HE 'S ALL THE WAY OUT TO LUNCH

   My Meaning: HE'S a NUT

5. What is? YOU CALLING ME OUT

   My Meaning: u wants to fight

1. What is? WHY BUY THE MILK WHEN HE GETTING THE WHOLE COW

    My Meaning: getting everything

2. What is? HOW CAN YOU LIVE WITH YOUSELF

    My Meaning: take a good look at who u r

3. What is? YOUR STIFF AS A BOARD

    My Meaning: move your ass

4. What is? GET THE HELL AWAY FROM ME

    My Meaning: don't look at me

5. What is? YOU KNOW WHAT AM TALKING ABOUT

    My Meaning: not hearing me

(Just a thought) CALL ME ANYTIME I BE WAITING

(just a thought)- Santa Claus comes straight to the hood- "for little children that believe in Santa Claus, you need to go straight to the hood. It's sad enough that the children, don't have a dream, hope, vision, and totally just take a Santa Claus gift or wish is a bad thing. So make a little boy or girl happy by giving a gift or present, clothes, food, shelter, love, comfort, protection, peace, and joy that there is good will toward man but most of all give them the true meaning of the holiday seasons it is not as much as the present but the presence of the spirit of Christmas. So don't forget the hood meaning every neighborhood where dreams are still alive.

(Just a thought) "What's going on with my mail?"

Will somebody please tell me what's going on with my mail? Well if it isn't one thing it's another, the mail man said "the door was locked" "I couldn't get in" "the package was delivered" "the post office says you need ID" "the address is not right". But people are stealing mail everyday without ID. Stealing checks from other people, packages, and personal belongings. What the hell is going on with my mail? The postal service need to get on their jobs as long as it takes to retrieve your mail. How could you fly there in two days and deliver it yourself, GET ON YOUR JOB! This is not the pony express. I want my damn mail on time! And secure, come on people handle your business, everybody else have too.

(Just a thought)- Someone said niggers are just like roaches; everywhere you go there is one right around the corner

If I can have my flowers while I am alive, I can enjoy them , see them, hold them , smell them , display them while they last ,not only physical flowers but spiritual flowers do me right treat me with love and respect now, hold me , hug me , kiss me tell me that I am beautiful ,that you appreciate that you care for me ,that I am important to you , that I count somewhere in this God forsaken world, so if you really love me like you say you do don't just say it with your words or mouths show me with your hearts , body, mind, and spirit .

Thanks

I thank you for being so good to me , loving, taking care of me ,protecting keeping me being their for (me)in my (darkness hour) understanding me inspire of my shortcomings , you are my sunshine on(rainy days) you are my warmth when I feel cold despair you're my friend in a time of need my mother, father, bother sister , when it seem know one understand or care , but you do so think you again even for being their for me when sometimes it seems like I am standing alone (I know it not true) thanks, thanks and many and many more to yo

www.ingramcontent.com/pod-product-compliance
Lightning Source LLC
Chambersburg PA
CBHW081424280526
45788CB00009B/3221